101 Uses for Gr

C000027175

Mogul

&

CLYDE

Take That Books is an imprint of
Take That Ltd.
P.O.Box 200
Harrogate
HG1 4XB

Copyright © 1993 Take That Books

10 9 8 7 6 5 4 3 2 1

All rights reserved around the world. This publication is copyright and may not be reproduced in whole or in part in
any manner (except excerpts thereof for bona fide purposes in accordance with the Copyright Act)
without the prior consent in writing from the publisher.

This is a work of humour and of fiction. Under no circumstances should anybody act on material given in this book.
The publisher, author, and their respective employees or agents, shall not accept responsibility for injury, loss or damage
occasioned by any person acting or refraining from action as a result of material in this book whether or not
such injury, loss or damage is in any way due to any negligent act or omission, breach of duty or
default on the part of the publisher, author, or their respective employees or agents.

ISBN 1-873668-06-6

Layout, illustrations and typesetting by Impact Design, P.O.Box 200, Harrogate, HG1 4XB.

Printed and bound in Great Britain.

TAKE THAT BOOKS

Ship's Figurehead

Lampstand

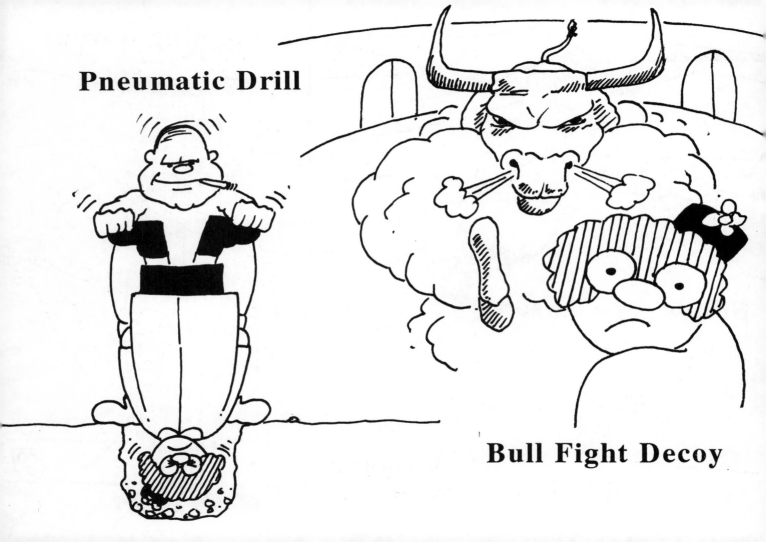

Ski Slalom pole

Juggling Baton

Mine Detector

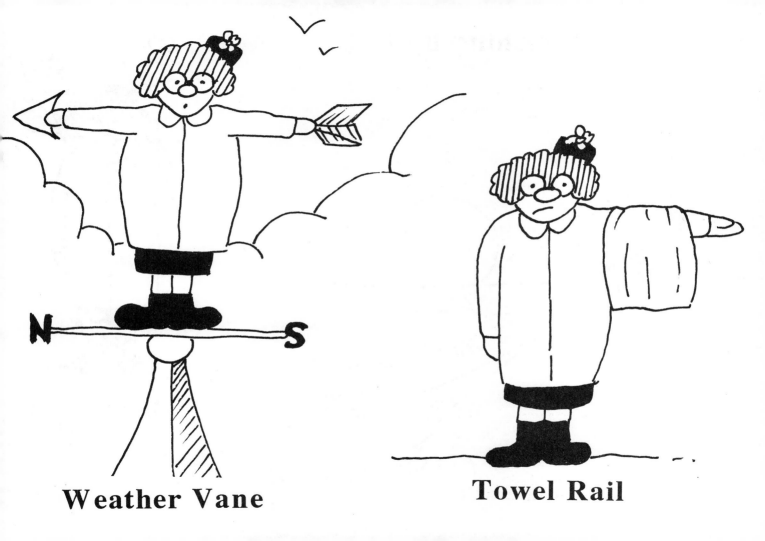

Weather Vane

Towel Rail

Axe

Outboard Motor

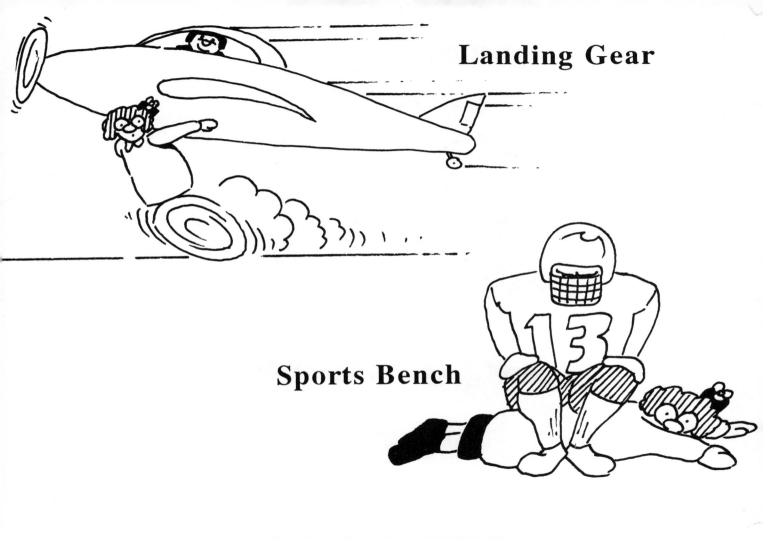

Garden Trestle

Hat Stand

Davy Lamp

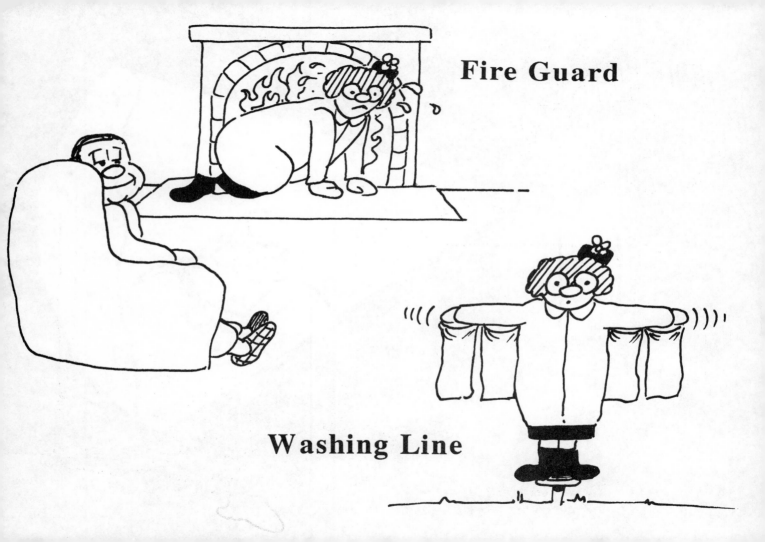

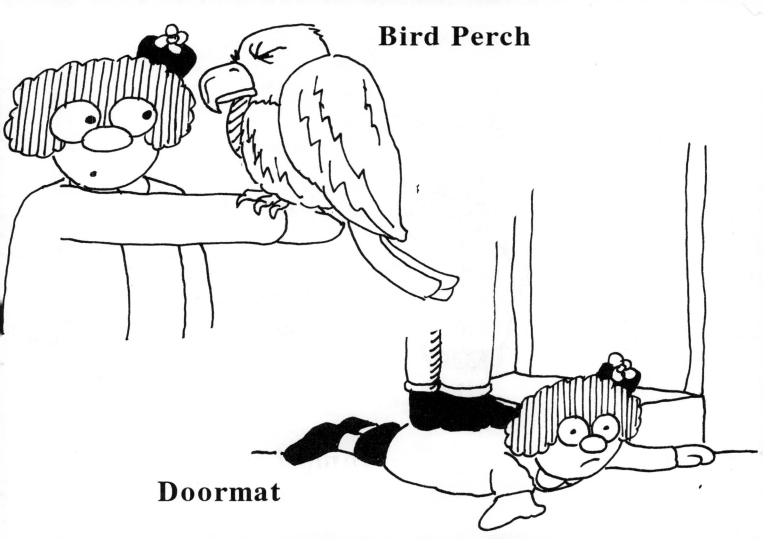

Jump Lead

Wind Sock

Window Cleaner's Basket

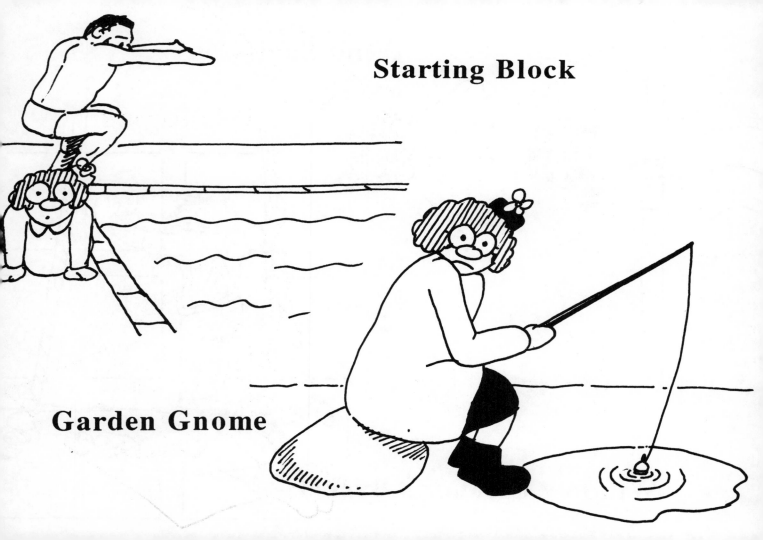

Starting Block

Garden Gnome

Scarecrow

Paint Brush

Dart Board

Summit Marker

Basketball

Candle Holder

Anchor

Kite

Sherpa

Buoy

Bumper

Mouse-trap

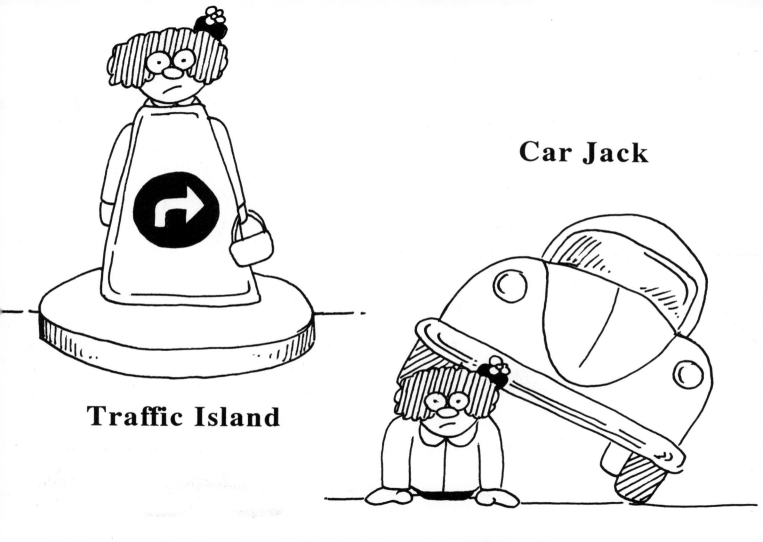

Traffic Island

Car Jack

Rocket

TV Aerial

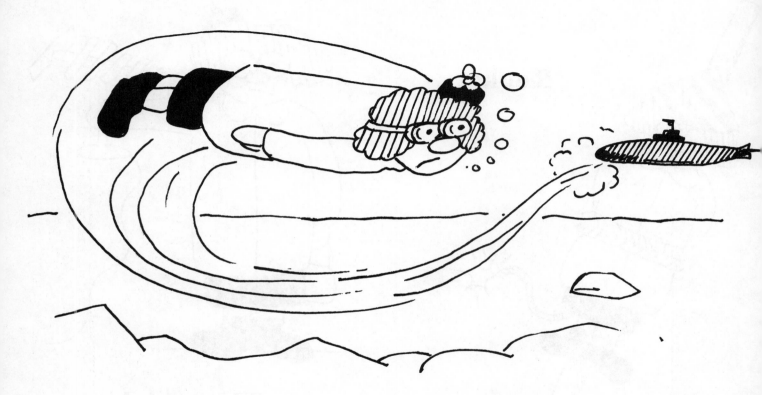

Torpedo

Bike Rack

Dog Treat

Satellite

Guard Dog

Stunt Granny

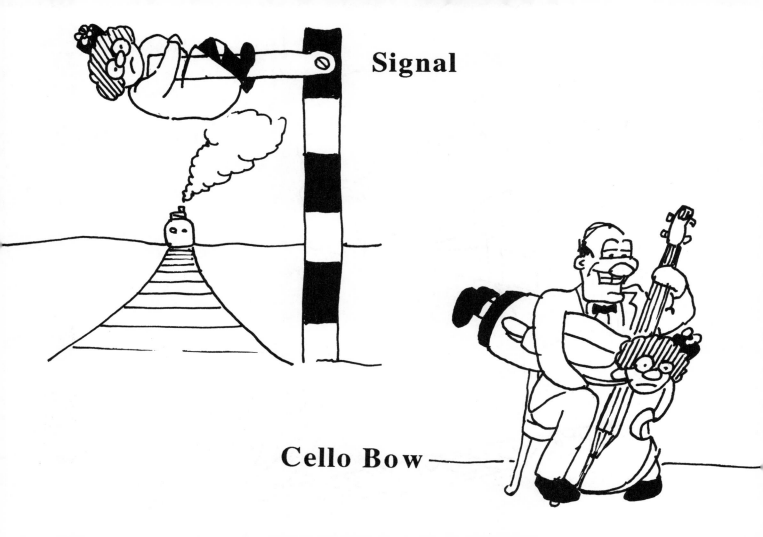

Cow-catcher

Baton

Drum Kit

Plumb Line

Hang-glider

Mower

Propeller

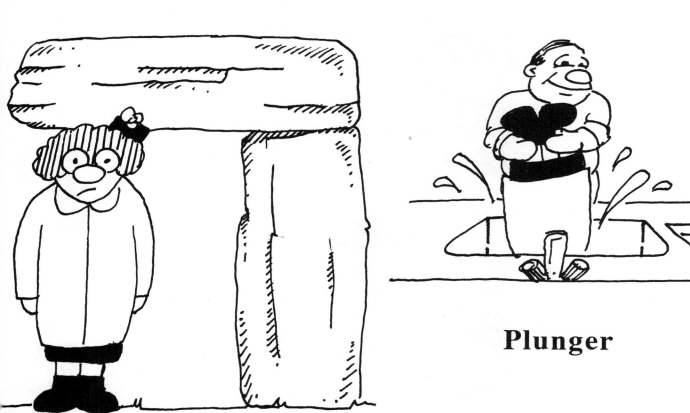

Ancient Monument

Plunger

Weights

Goal Post

Husky

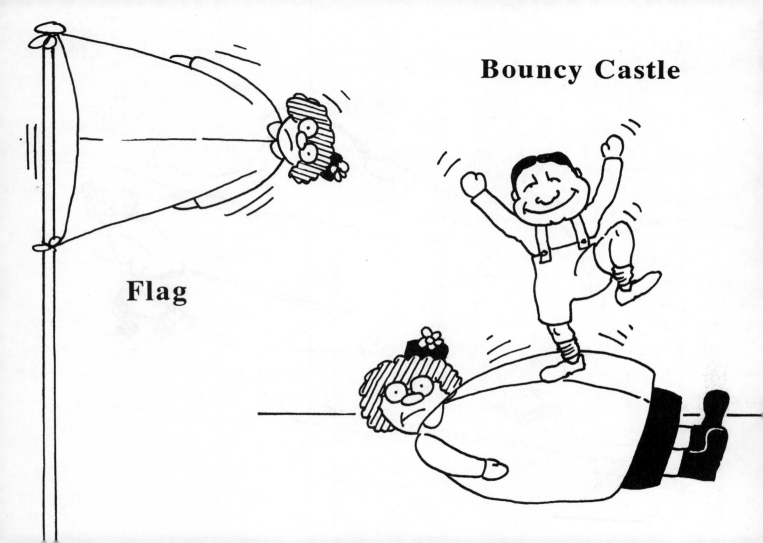

Flag

Bouncy Castle

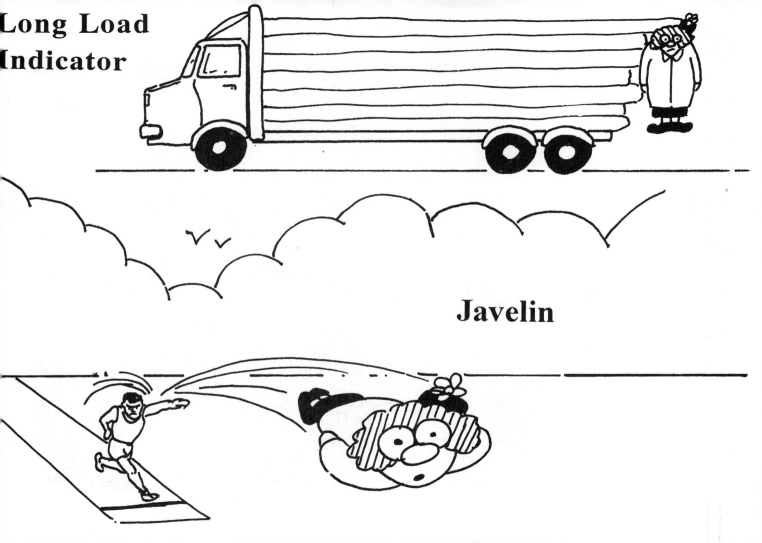

Long Load Indicator

Javelin

Sleeping Policeman

Chimney Sweep

Letter Rack

Tourist Attraction

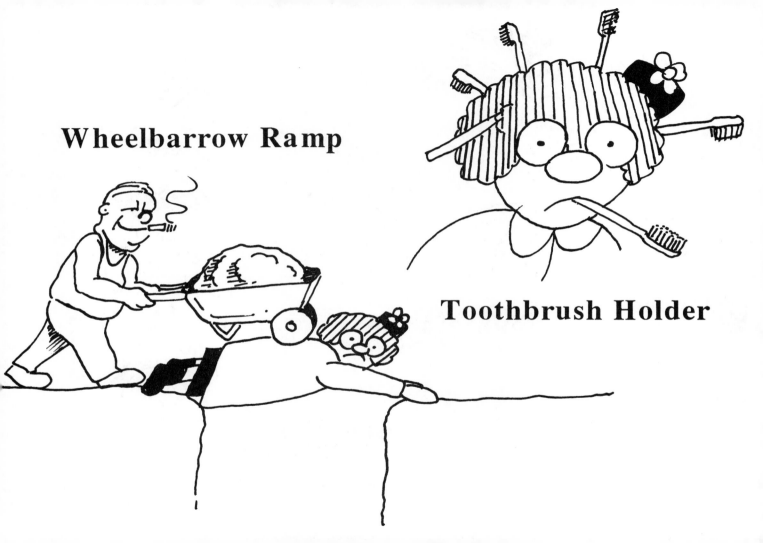

Wheelbarrow Ramp

Toothbrush Holder

Fountain

Totem Pole

Water Ski

Sledge

Brick Hod

Snooker Cue

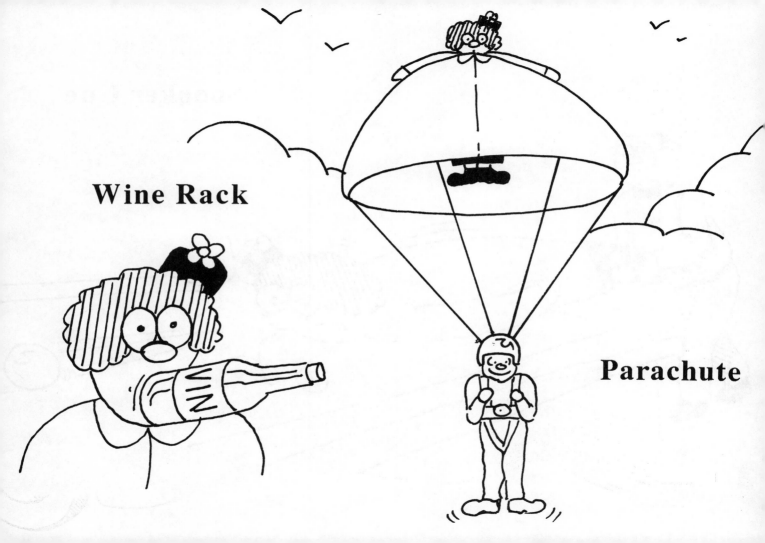

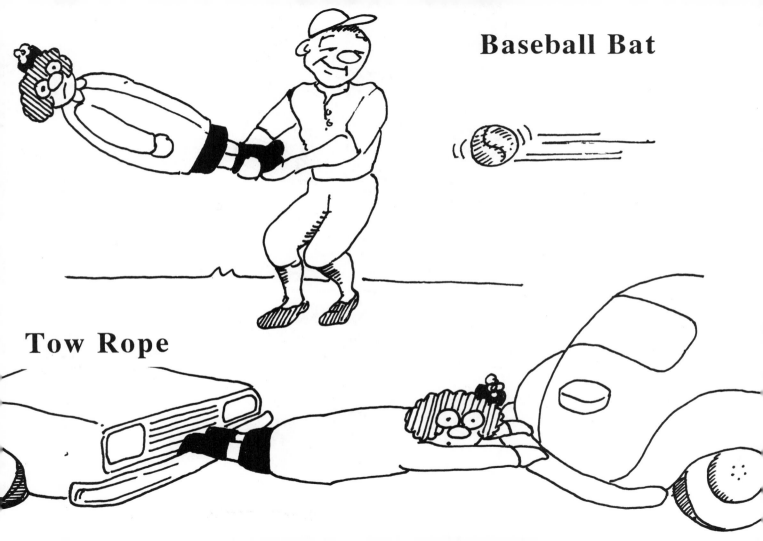

Baseball Bat

Tow Rope

Rugby Ball

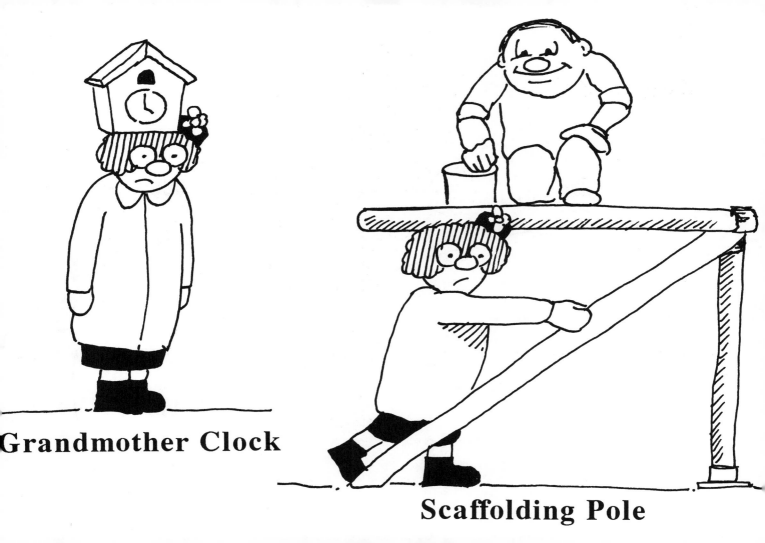

Grandmother Clock

Scaffolding Pole

Canoe Paddle

Bird Table